PROGRESS ON THE SUBJECT OF IMMENSITY

MARY BURRITT CHRISTIANSEN POETRY SERIES
Hilda Raz, Series Editor

Also available in the University of New Mexico Press Mary Burritt Christiansen Poetry Series:

Mary Burritt
Christiansen
Poetry Series

Poets of the Non-Existent City: Los Angeles in the McCarthy Era, edited by Estelle Gershgoren Novak

Selected Poems of Gabriela Mistral, edited by Ursula K. Le Guin

Deeply Dug In by R. L. Barth

Amulet Songs: Poems Selected and New by Lucile Adler

In Company: An Anthology of New Mexico Poets After 1960, edited by Lee Bartlett, V. B. Price, and Dianne Edenfield Edwards

Tiempos Lejanos: Poetic Images from the Past by Nasario García

Refuge of Whirling Light by Mary Beath

The River Is Wide/El río es ancho: Twenty Mexican Poets, a Bilingual Anthology, edited and translated by Marlon L. Fick

A Scar Upon Our Voice by Robin Coffee

CrashBoomLove: A Novel in Verse by Juan Felipe Herrera

In a Dybbuk's Raincoat: Collected Poems by Bert Meyers

Rebirth of Wonder: Poems of the Common Life by David M. Johnson

Broken and Reset: Selected Poems, 1966 to 2006 by V. B. Price

The Curvature of the Earth by Gene Frumkin and Alvaro Cardona-Hine

Derivative of the Moving Image by Jennifer Bartlett

Map of the Lost by Miriam Sagan

¿de Veras?: Young Voices from the National Hispanic Cultural Center, edited by Mikaela Jae Renz and Shelle VanEtten-Luaces

A Bigger Boat: The Unlikely Success of the Albuquerque Poetry Slam Scene, edited by Susan McAllister, Don McIver, Mikaela Renz, and Daniel S. Solis

A Poetry of Remembrance: New and Rejected Works by Levi Romero

The Welcome Table by Jay Udall

How Shadows Are Bundled by Anne Valley-Fox

Bolitas de oro: Poems of My Marble-Playing Days by Nasario García

Blood Desert: Witnesses, 1820–1880 by Renny Golden

The Singing Bowl by Joan Logghe

Ruins by Margaret Randall

Begging for Vultures by Lawrence Welsh

Breaths by Eleuterio Santiago-Díaz

City of Slow Dissolve by John Chávez

Losing the Ring in the River by Marjorie Saiser

Say That by Felecia Caton Garcia

Flirt by Noah Blaustein

PROGRESS ON THE SUBJECT OF
IMMENSITY

Leslie Ullman

UNIVERSITY OF NEW MEXICO PRESS
ALBUQUERQUE

All rights reserved. Published 2013
Printed in the United States of America
18 17 16 15 14 13   1 2 3 4 5 6

Library of Congress Cataloging-in-Publication Data
Ullman, Leslie.
 [Poems. Selections]
 Progress on the subject of immensity / Leslie Ullman.
     pages ; cm. — (Mary Burritt Christiansen poetry series)
 Includes bibliographical references.
 ISBN 978-0-8263-5362-7 (pbk. : alk. paper) — ISBN 978-0-8263-5363-4 (electronic)
 I. Title.
 PS3571.L57P76 2013
 811'.54—dc23

                              2013004418

TEXT COMPOSED BY CATHERINE LEONARDO
Composed in Dante MT Std 11.5/13.5
Display type is Dante MT Std

Contents

Acknowledgments   vii

I

Abrupt at Dawn   3
Undertow   4
Ice Apples   5
Equinox   7
The Guises of the Mind   9
Mind Outside   10
Don't Sleep Yet   11
Mind Undressed   12
The Story I Need   13
Water Music   14
Before They Plowed the Orchard Under   16
Spacious   17
Beautiful / This Morning, No Myth Felt Lacking,   18
Night Opens the Foothills   19
Password   21

II

Against Diffuse Awareness   25
Mind Without Instruments in Low Visibility   27
Vespers, 1961   28
Almost Listening . . .   29
By Night, Penelope   30
Amnesia   31
Mind Paces the Edge of a Flat World   32

Moon, Shrinking   33
Cloud   34
Zone by Zone   35
Conviction   36
History of Art in the Twenty-First Century   37
Contract   39
Among the Mysteries   41
Equatorial   43
And My Life Wandered On   45
Mind Returns to Find Itself Absent   46

III

Mind Trades Shadows with the Clouds   49
Patient   51
At the End of Daylight Savings   52
Hole in the Mind Filling with the Present   53
A Visible Life   54
Mind Out of Season   55
The Seasons Only Borrow Us   56
Progress on the Subject of Immensity   57
Mind Gives Up an Attempt to
    Describe the Scent of New Paper   59
Nova That Suddenly   60
Without Steel or Fire   61
Mudra   62
Two   63
Still, Small   64
Consider Desire   65

Notes   67

Acknowledgments

I am grateful to the following publications in which these poems first appeared:

Alabama Literary Review: "At the End of Daylight Savings"
Arts & Letters: "Mind Returns to Find Itself Absent" and "Mind Outside"
BorderSenses: "Undertow" (under the title "Via Fortuda")
The Cape Rock: "Nova That Suddenly"and "Before They Plowed the Orchard Under"
Cerise Press: "The Story I Need"
The Chariton Review: "Password" and "Cloud"
Chokecherries: "A Visible Life," "Conviction," and "Moon Shrinking"
The Cincinnati Review: "Mind Undressed"
decomP: "Ice Apples"
Ecotone: "Equatorial"
Forge: "Contract"
Green Mountains Review: "Two"
Iron Horse Literary Review: "Equinox," "Progress on the Subject of Immensity" (under the title "Sky: An Inquiry"), *"Beautiful / This Morning No Myth Felt Lacking"* (under the title "Each Wave a Bit of Wind"), and "Water Music"
The MacGuffin: "By Night, Penelope"
New Letters: "History of Art in the Twenty-First Century" (under the title "History of Art in the 21st Century")
Numéro Cinq: "Almost Listening . . . ," *"Don't Sleep Yet,"* and "Consider Desire"
Pembroke Magazine: "Abrupt at Dawn," "The Guises of the Mind," and "Mind Without Instruments in Low Visibility"
Poet Lore: "And My Life Wandered On"
The Poetry Miscellany: "Against Diffuse Awareness"
Río Grande Review: "Without Steel or Fire"
Saranac Review: "Hole in the Mind Filling with the Present"

Shenandoah: "Spacious" and "Night Opens the Foothills"

Smartish Pace: "Mind Trades Shadows with the Clouds"

Solstice Literary Magazine: "Zone by Zone," "The Seasons Only Borrow Us," and "Mind Gives Up an Attempt to Describe the Scent of New Paper" (under the title "Mind Gives Up the Attempt to Describe the Scent of New Paper")

Southwestern American Literature: "Mind Paces the Edge of a Flat World"

TEX!: "Among the Mysteries"

The Texas Review: "Patient"

Special thanks to the Wurlitzer Foundation and Hedgebrook for their generous gifts of time, solitude, and just the right amount of fellowship.

Thanks also to friends who have read my work and shared theirs: Kathleen Condon, Sandra Blystone, Sharon Owen, Robin Scofield, Judith Rice, Andrea Watson, Veronica Golos, Judith Thompson, Betsy Sholl, and Dave Jauss.

I

Abrupt at Dawn

I was sure the sound
of engines came from
inside me, thrum of labors
that had driven me
in and out of sleep.
And then coyotes, scores
of them, sent out
ribbons of sound strangely
close to the house—something
disembodied, metallic,
the high, shrill gears
adding to whatever the sun
was using to ratchet itself up.
I pictured them seated squarely
on the ground, their cries
thrust from inside like projectiles,
their eyes half-closed—perhaps
the sound was their way of releasing
whatever the night had left
unfinished in them, whatever
kept them prowling. I don't know
what made them start
so suddenly and then stop,
leaving a thing that quivered
in the air. Leaving the neighbors' dogs
tangled in their own barking.

Now, winter sage outside my window
trembles, bends and springs back
and bends again, and I realize
the first sound I heard was wind
blowing in a front. The machinery
of real weather. And I am simply
in its path like any creature,
not wrongly placed,
though the day, like a boat
in hard sea, churns
so fiercely beneath me.

Undertow

Through the sluggish dawns
of December, the river slows
in our sleep, its summer currents
drained and stalled to pools. We rise
to familiar torpor. But the horses
will go in if we nudge with our legs
and wait—nudge again and keep their
heads pointed at the drop. A halt,
a slide, then a leap—they are unsure
and exultant. We guide them
in and out until they don't stop
but let faith carry them clean
over the bank. Full of themselves, now
they take their bits and hurl us with them
through mud and water, the underworld
that keeps slipping with each foothold.
They beat the stagnant water
to a froth, they spray us with
shards of our waking dreams
that vanished when light returned.
We can't stop—or even slow down—
so we aim along a string of sandbars
in and out of icy water,
the lick of winter, the doubt
that settled in our sleep—
and get used to not knowing
how deep it will be until we are in it.

Ice Apples

The aspen once lit from inside
stripped of their startled gold,
fallen glints of geranium
tamped to mulch and snowfall,
the late-ripened apples locked in ice—
these arctic nights, we are thrown back
on ourselves by what has been
taken away. It seems always

to be night. We find ourselves dozing
in a cave of sofa and muted TV sounds,
a book left open on the armrest
and another on a vacant cushion, the room
not so much warm as a neutral zone
in the chill advancing like a phalanx
bent on more than plunder. The cessation
of consciousness. We drift in and out

of memory that is less event
than atmosphere—the alertness,
a pastel wash with bold strokes
of umber when love first arrives,
and the greater alertness—burnished
gold behind the eyes, dark grooves
celebrating the texture—when it leaves
yet again, innocence and experience

etching those repetitions that keep us
from becoming, even briefly, truly fallow
as the pull of what could be coming next
keeps undoing the seams between
grey spirit and gravity. In this, our
hibernation is uniquely human.
Few would call it a journey. Few
would say that at such times

we are accompanied, losing a self
in inner rooms that keep expanding
as another, then another self fills them—
think of Magritte's huge apple
disembodied, all flesh, seeds, and light
played out in paint, touching every
wall in an ordinary room as though it had
flowed in like the sun.

Equinox

Who will buy me an orange
to console me now?
Who will tempt me with
a handful of fireflies
or fine white sand?
Who will come to the edge
of this water, the drop
to its invisible floor, and wave
a bouquet of iris before me—who

will fill my eyes with blue light?
Water, black water
has turned to ice and lulled
the long valley into a doze—soon
we'll all sprout gills, drifting
in a sleep beyond memory,
beyond the residual lung,
beyond the spent coals

of desire. But that first
drop of juice—so
sweet-startling—a sacrament—
light in a throat from which
song has nearly faded—
could it guide me back
to shore? An orange, small sun
dawning from the inside
to resurrect the mammal body

limb by limb. . . . Even now
I'm saying a silent
yes, teaching myself
to behold it without a twinge
of winter in my shoulders. Without
cringing from the space
I consider taking once again

in the famished world. One day
I will reach, the sun warming the pale
skin of my wrist as silt falls away—
and for a moment your orange will be
suspended between us, perfectly cherished.

The Guises of the Mind

relinquished long ago their faux fur
and studded shoes, their tattoos and lacquers,
now their fortified bone mass and lubricated joints.
Cannot be used to heat a room, polish leather,
or cut stone. They cast no shadow but think
they do. Have never lost themselves to passion
they never grasped anyway, squinting through
reading glasses and smoky footlights.
Are cracked plaster. Clogged gutters.
Seeds the birds have left behind.
Decals easy to peel from the hearts of those
who've tried to love them.

Every morning they wake startled
and inexplicably frightened. They push their
tailored, obedient selves into cubicles
and conference rooms. They retain
no scent, can neither be traced nor followed,
can neither be made nor unmade.
Are more lucid in their sleep, which is shallow,
than over double espresso in the sun.
Have no patience for fine print. Are creatures of habit
until the doctor reveals troubled maps inside.

How they clomp through the wild flowers and thick
grasses of August—they might as well be crossing
hot asphalt against traffic. They can't remain
still enough to feel the slow ripening that could
be theirs—the nectar turning, beneath a thickened
rind, its stored sugars to the late October sun.
They've never let grief spear them and have its way
before moving on; every one of them pounds
and pounds at the door of the one house
that won't accept them, the one heart, the one
indifferent ear—willful, running on fumes,
they throw themselves against that hardness.

Mind Outside

The sun rises heavily to dissolve
the dreamed barn
and an imaginary nearness of
mountains. The half-grown colt
begins to pace the immense
new field; he doesn't know
which fence means home,
which of the older horses
will befriend him. Their hooves press
scar after scar into damp ground.
Their teeth tear grass at the root.
Sunlight flashes off his white-rimmed eyes
as he backs away; not today
will he stand rump to nose with them,
holding flies at bay, or lie down beside them
as they turn one side to the sun
and the other to a silent,
knowable earth.

Don't Sleep Yet

This is what you've longed for,
drops tapping the shingles
and the silent flowering of each word
printed on the page before you.
Water pours off the eaves and drips
into the dead leaves outside, and you
are held, held the way wood and glass
were meant to hold you. Keep
the rain. You need the privacy
tomorrow will shred to bits. Blue
rain. Streaked wind. The lamp
pulling the room around it. The book
pulling your life around it. The rain
is trying to tell you a story
of going outside and
coming back in.

Mind Undressed

Do you need the perfume
called Lotus Flower? The yellowed
plumage of a gown you wore
only once? The cushion of money
waiting for you to fall upon hard times?

And those stones
you borrowed from several rivers—
the one layered with little caves,
the white oval,
the one with a hole at one end, all of them
gathered those years when you thought

they spoke to you,
when you thought they asked
to follow you inland, to your
bare windowsills and desk—
let them go back underwater
to continue their own slow stories.

Wait, as the sun edges closer
to your throat, for the voices
you've honed and fed all these years
to return to their river as well. Wait
for the silence that will not eat
if you try to feed it, will not stay
if you pretend it isn't there—

name it the light side of the dark moon
you have been. Go ahead and confuse it
with the sun that touches you
everywhere at once.

The Story I Need

Ah, if only the village were so small,
and I could look into others' windows by
looking into my own cupped hands

to see what steams on their
plates, or read the spines of books
on their shelves—all those lives

to open one at a time—I might hold
the history of civilization a little closer
to my own small history—bread
passed down from the centuries, boots
on cobblestone, couples' first words

in the morning—not for the privacies
but as proof of the way buildings hold the countless
small movements of words and bodies
through space, and for the feeling

that I, too, am drying the cups and putting them away
or sitting at the tavern, a chessboard
open between me and the oldest inhabitant

or joining a family at their picnic in the sun,
unable to distinguish myself from
the murmuring parents and noisy siblings
gathered around the cheese and pears
they have chosen, in a world

of possibilities, to set on the bright cloth.

Water Music

I have fashioned a miniature fountain
from scraps of dream—
palm-sized pump, Steuben glass bowl
kept in its box twenty-five years,
rocks collected in a rain hat
from the beach at Normandy. I settle
beside it, in my house, hearing
the echo of tides that licked those rocks
one way, then another, a sound
that makes me long to be
touched by upheaval. History
bearing me somewhere I haven't been.
History raking my skin and leaving
some ghost of the world's grief, wise
and luminous in my gaze

despite the old distractions—swing music,
heirloom silver, a rose by the bed, the trance
of courtship. . . . Yet when I read the great
poems written by men who lived
before me, I find myself peering through
museum glass, waiting to be allowed
inside. Then outside. Against the rigors
that might forge and pound into shape
a significant life, there is something else
I crave—maybe grace, a sense of my feet
caressing the ground—that only
seems irrelevant, the way a child's humming
might be when she thinks herself
unobserved, playing among wild flowers,
or the way some men's faces soften

when they dance, their hands
light and aware at a woman's waist
and shoulder. One shrugs off the entire
weight of the Presbyterian Church

as he glides into a rumba; another teases
his partner toward him and away
like a cape; another just lowers his eyes,
smiles through half-moon lids
and seems to float out of his body altogether
as he keeps himself and his partner in perfect frame—
when their hips give in to the music
and I can see in their faces the world's business
has loosened its hold, how can I not love them,
how can I think my minor note
unaccompanied?

Before They Plowed the Orchard Under

Every fall the branches were jeweled with
warm, fist-sized apples we could pick from horseback
though we lived in the desert, which may explain
the barely perceptible sweetness of their flesh.
Nicky ate hers out of my hand—each apple in two neat bites.

Late autumn into winter, the whole ranch smelled
of windfalls and sun, amber fermenting
and seeping into the sand as though into a tavern's
old wood floor—I felt giddy each time I drove home
through the early dusk, rolling down my window

though it wouldn't be until spring, when the river
filled the ditches and the trees released a froth of white
and pink against the grey mountains, that their own
celebration, saved for the new season, made them
sway all night in their plumage, their drinking songs.

Spacious

The cycles of sowings and harvests
in the fields, and her own body moving easily
in and out of the weather. Her parents
still themselves in their glowing home
far away, poised to welcome her.
Sometimes the memory of another house

and the sullen silences that filled it
and the abandoned water tower behind it
where she sneaked away after quarrels
to weep alone, old at thirty.
Now her will sails on, nothing
to impede it, as the men, even the ones

who've done the leaving—a lover
damaged by divorce, a lover damaged
by war—shrink far behind.
Even the two horses seem to
linger in their long prime,
the bellied sling of these middle years.

The rhythms of the fields.
Her small, solid house.
Some evenings a run in the fading light.
Or dancing, then driving home alone
and happy, sweat drying under the sequins.

Beautiful / This Morning, No Myth Felt Lacking,

my shirt and trousers faded
to the greys of sea,
the doorway I lean against,
an arch of silvered wood.
My bare feet press swells of sand
and crushed shells on their way
to water—we massage each other,
my feet and this beach, each changing
the surface of the other. Each wave
is a bit of wind riding

the earth's long curve—
no myth felt lacking in the waves'
conversation with shore,
no myth felt lacking in the house,
its doors open to waves that breathe
fine salt into the grain of
the table, into cotton garments
drying on the line. I sleep
in a gown full of sun. I drink
from a bucket of rain. I eat slices of sun
one by one as I peel an orange
and I eat its earth skin too.

The waves' hush, rhythmic and
round, is the sound of breath passing
from belly to throat—if I listen
long enough, it turns to
a word now and then, a phrase, as though
someone inside me were trying to speak
gently of skin that bakes to leather,
of silver that crinkles the hair, of a body
turning to driftwood in a doorway
whose threshold I cross countless times a day,
even when standing still.

Night Opens the Foothills

I walk through the house, turning off
every lamp but one, leaving
a trail of small relinquishments—

a book turned facedown
at the spot where sleepiness overtook
the little cogs and wheels,

a cup of tea tasted and then forgotten.
What has not been accomplished

lingers as restlessness that braids
itself into my imperfect
sleep, the cogs and wheels of dreams

and now the house and all the other houses
strung along the seams of the valley are left

to themselves. The words spoken inside them
all day, the air displaced from objects

lifted and set down, and the scents of onion
or lemon oil settle into paper, into cloth,
between grains of polished wood. Each house

breathes on its own now, the sound of
water staying warm in its tank.

The mountain melts into the night, veiled
and uninhabited. An altar. A silence.
The houses meld into the mountain

in that most private hour just before
dawn sets every timber and stone, every
roof, every dish and birdcall back into place.

In that most private hour, I heat
the coffee and some mornings
find myself reading of other lives

as the sun inches toward plums
in a white bowl. The ceramic glaze
of the cup. They could be stones resting

in a clear stream, bathed in the silence
of another kind of morning

absorbed and given purpose:
stones to be shaped and fitted for
a cathedral, bone needles

pulled along seams of broadcloth
as the nuns' way of listening to their God

and bread broken and passed around,
breaking a fast that once sharpened, as it
sharpens still, the colors and contours

of faith, and savored as though nothing
at the moment could be more desired.

Password

One night I slept without

dreaming, as though restlessness
had found another sleeper
to ravage. Someone else's
memories, jagged, waiting to be
turned up and plowed under.
Next morning, I found myself
picking up books and putting them down,
for once not straining to harvest some
sign meant especially for me
from the venerable lines. I kept waiting
for a task to announce itself, to pull me in
and set the frantic clock going again.

In those blank hours, elsewhere, change
undoubtedly occurred—a field of seed pods
lifting on a single strip of wind,
a row of bulbs sealing themselves
against crisp nights for the months
of their own sleep. . . . My eyes
drifted inward, lazily, as though
merging with the sky. Something, warm
cotton, seemed to have closed in, holding me
like a hand cupped gently. So I entered
my sixty-first year. An absence
not necessarily without promise.

A turned field.

II

Against Diffuse Awareness

Do not speculate on the destination of
the plastic bag blowing across the parking lot
or how the queen-sized mattress ended up on the freeway.

Do not let your mind stray, midway
between freezer and microwave, to
contemplate how every gadget in your
kitchen, every digital number
and bleep, has been extracted from rock
or water. Vanished fire. Wind.

Do not dwell on random motion, wave–particle
duality, thermodynamics, or any other
commotion going on in the air you breathe,
the water that runs over your hands,
transformations ubiquitous and fleeting as the glint
of a shod hoof disappearing in the sun.

Do not stare into vacant lots in the middle of cities
like Chicago, with their bald spots and empty cartons
and weeds gone out of control, each detail
a whole genealogy of neglect—or try to
imagine the vast roots that once reigned there
as branches held their poise, like the arms
of flamenco dancers, in hard rain.

Do not pause at the sound of someone
weeping quietly—say, behind a newspaper
on the train, in a phone booth, or in a restroom stall—
as each exhalation, having gathered itself
from a rare moment of communion
with the soul (which for that moment is not
an abstraction), suspends itself.

Forget this story—just one of many crowding
the dumping grounds of what you insist

you don't have time for—about a peasant
who helped build the great cathedral at Chartres,
who sluiced dirt from his tired body one evening
and stood before his hut, letting his mind
roam with the crickets and sheep. As the stars
faded, his thoughts lifted him
from himself and set him down
as rough quarried stone. Gold
in the priest's coffers. Prayer on the lips
of a new widow. Light still glimmering in the passage
etched behind the eyes of his newborn son
who, in his own lifetime, would not see the cathedral finished.

Mind Without Instruments in Low Visibility

Stones come alive
everywhere, when early sun
makes them gleam against the still-
darkened ground. Each holds secrets
longer than the history of imagination.

Throughout the day a word might
slip beyond the speaker's intentions
but remain disguised as a recognizable
set of possibilities; so the rogue's *I*
is a seductive *you*, and the betrayed
lover's *you*, the *us* that razes
the betrayer's heart. . . . Other utterances slip

out of hiding from a pocket or drawer—requests
for funds from an agency holding slender
hands against a dyke about to be breached;
directions jotted hastily and with real intent
to a house (but whose?); a name
floating alone on a napkin, as though released
from a bottle but still traveling.

Fresh-picked carrots, trailing midnight
from slender tendrils, offer a sudden
flash of something besides
color: Silence. Spears of sun.
Raspberries, shut in freezers for weeks
and thawed in a white bowl, release the trapped
taste of a particular noon in August

even as the literal sun goes down in a new place
every evening, taking with it the noise of
workmen repairing a neighbor's roof.
The air tightens for winter; soon each house
stays dim well into the morning. Mind peers
over the brim of the realm of no words,
drops into a longing that waits
where light has never been, then drops
down further.

Vespers, 1961

From pine and birch, the multitudes
of full-summer greens, birds
wove a trellis of song, all light
and air. God was mentioned, but He
was superfluous. All summer, the trees
had been drinking what they needed,
saving the dew for the smallest
creatures and thirsty air,
and no native plant or animal wished
to be elsewhere. Even the birds
seemed held in the pause
of Sabbath, and not one of us girls
was restless or distracted as we sang hymns
our upbringings may not have approved.
We were Peter Pan's lost
and lucky children, made new
by the summer-long absence of boys, TV,
full-length mirrors, and junk food,
though we had arrived teetering
at the brink of experiment.
Each Sunday we washed our hair in the lake
and donned clean white blouses
and shorts. Our church clothes.
The lake flashed its gentle mirror through the trees
and beyond it, our lives waited
to take on glitter. To deepen and tarnish.
To drive us to seek in vain
what terms we could find for perfection.

Almost Listening . . .

Not *revelation* shot from the hip
by the mind practicing its aim
on the future, or *fact* the mind
wields like a mallet, never waiting
to see what wing-fragile contours
it might settle around, never accepting or
offering it as a handful of water that holds
its shape even as some leaks between the fingers

the truth, as *incipience*,
is rarely allowed to slip into the ear of someone

in the street, talking rapidly into an invisible
phone as though talking to himself,
or to settle beside him in the airport lounge
as he taps money and one-liners into
his keyboard; is rarely glimpsed
by the young mother rushing in shoes
that pinch, after hours of setting plates before others,
toward the aluminum glare of the bus

she may miss; is rarely allowed *presence*
like a word thought before it is spoken

or a note that is less sound than an exhalation
riding the air from another latitude
long after it has signaled, from a burnished
gong, the end of a ritual meditation

or like the fur of an animal camouflaged
amid dark trees on a moonless night,
a large animal believed to be dangerous
when removed from his world, or when his world
is altered by our presence in it.

By Night, Penelope

unstitches the shoreline, the sea, the barely
visible mountain—all that binds her
to her halted story and to the suitors
who dwell below her chamber,
banging their goblets and cursing.
She unstitches the lambs being driven
single-file toward the banquet table.
She unstitches her flesh so that it rises, freed
from its single allegiance, the marriage bed
that would hand her like a birthright
to one of the next ones circling,
waiting to be chosen. She unstitches
their tunics while they sleep and piles them
like shrouds over the wine-drugged bodies.

Pulling jeweled threads from the sunrise
and later from amethyst twilight
she adds them to a garment all her own,
a cloak of breath, silk, all the hues
of weather, a cloak that bears her aloft
on what will later be understood as the beam
of meditation—each night she is swift
and ambrosial, her tears sweetening the torn
fields, the blood-dark seas, Cyclops' cratered eye.
Sometimes, from the depths of his own stupor
far away, Odysseus hears a curious singing or keening
that would press him toward a boundary
he cannot yet imagine, between his headlong quest
and the apparent stillness of the earth's flanks and inland waters.

Amnesia

From the foliage a whistling—people or birds?
　　　　　　　　—Tomas Tranströmer

Then the lull as Earth
seems to stall before turning
again toward the sun. Sometimes the silence
is so absolute as to be unbreathable,
a flutter of panicked wings in the chest
or the ear simply hearing itself—
the crescendo of birth
underwater, song of growing
nerve and bone, filament and swirl
and, finally, the letting-in of air,
though the ear never let seawater
escape entirely from its spiral caves—
perhaps what we hear is our fear
of drowning.

We've learned to love our cities
for their hard lines and vertical walls,
their clash of locks and bodies, their glare,
their appetites, their never-sleep.
We've learned to mistake them
for harbor. While the earth barely
puts up with us, holding back
what it can, and the sky is an element
we muscle through, graceless
and afraid, in a crush of noise
and fuel. It never holds us for long.
Once we hacked our way to the asphalt
we could go no further. And the sea
would not receive us again.

Mind Paces the Edge of a Flat World

Savior and Satan could be
two sides of one
easy out. Either way
we give allegiance to
an element that may
be space, may be force,
or both, like those small
and large spirals of air that lift
another layer from the earth's skin
on their way somewhere else.
Eventually, everything
must land—La Virgen de Guadalupe
appears on a window shade
or a truck falls on someone's house
but most of it—the dust,
the tumbleweeds and dead
leaves, the jet streams
working inaccessible tracts of

water and land—who knows?
Every spring, the earth
offers something else
that's true, which includes
what died, what it surrendered,
what was ignored
so easily beneath snow
and the snow itself, which, even
in its season, was less
substance than a benign silence
that thickened and wove itself into
the diminished light
as each star nestled
in a blanket of others
before it warmed and sank
forever down—perhaps someday we'll
think twice before we
place footprints over a green
so fresh it seems part sun.

Moon, Shrinking

All the windows across the valley
have grown dark
near dawn, in the same
brief hour, dense as clapboard,

and certain grasses refuse to give up
their green, their version
of light, as the earth turns

away from the sun.
A hard frost. Another
vanished year. Fallen leaves soften
the roads as though preparing them for seed.

The waxing swelled
bit by bit with its future—light
of moonstone, light of calcite and pearl—

one season, clouds of moths
filling the house. Leaving brown smudges
on the ivory shades. You can't remember how
you got them out, or what their wings became part of.

Cloud

What could be taken for
compliance is not necessarily
its intention. It releases
any musings, such as they are,
to random winds. Dust and ozone
whistle through its open
doors and windows

even as it moves.

It empties and remains full—shouldn't rain
make it vanish?—allowing planes, whose silver
seems dark inside it, to pass through
briefly—perhaps it welcomes the chance to be
witnessed as the something
and nothing it is.

It is often mistaken for shade.

This cloud today is not an O'Keeffe
wash of cotton or a somber grey sponge
but a sheet spread thin by jet stream,
covering the whole sky, appearing
as a boundary between us and
everything else, the way a thought does
before another takes its place.

Zone by Zone

If noise could be experienced
as a form of light, daylight
no longer arrived as hard fact—
more like a window already open
that opened wider, allowing yesterday's
leftover clutter to flood back into our world.
The lights on coffeepots blinked on, small eyes,
as each day arranged itself into blocks
of sound: fluorescent skin, its pallor
hovering like exhaust over rows of desks,
phones and digital screens blinking in distress.

Respite, now and then, when the new leaf
on a begonia cutting unfolded visibly
in a cubicle window, or the colors in a partial
rainbow, almost imagined, grew
more intense as we moved through
new angles of light. Real silence

would not have rippled very far, small
pebble, as each of us, temporarily alone as we
drove home from work, navigated by way
of the *seek* button, replacing static with measured
voices, good diction, controlled renditions of
uncontrolled weather patterns, currencies, civilian
body counts, politicians frozen into stalemate. . . .

Thus did the usual first chords of National Public
five o'clock news, following the sun, deliver
each of us zone by zone into a familiar arrangement
of switches and lamps. The promise of spirits
on ice. Marking the boundary between
the tiny country of our days
and the tinier country of our evenings.

Conviction

Partial truth
is an act of closing
the throat—not
like sadness before it
moves on.

Cold rain. We arrive at another
hotel, stalled in what we
said yesterday, last week.
*Cliché. A rendition
of truth.* Exit. Cold rain.

No further comment   what we
          don't want to say
the order of the day   in quick succession
     on the turnpike   jumpy
in the back seat   until
                    everything but lights disappears

Sometimes we remember
what it felt like when it
passed through us, quick
and warm, the wipers
smearing leaves over the windshield. . . .
We saw horses running
in a line, for the joy of it, in their
emerald field of a home.

History of Art in the Twenty-First Century

We are descended from violence.
Along with the wheel and pulley,
the geometries of Stonehenge, the metate,
the amphora and the vaulted ceiling, we've
left pillage along the trade routes. Skulls
of the conquered strung along poles. Evidence
of human flesh processed with stone tools
and thrown into boiling water. This recently
has been revealed, despite our objections,
by carbon dating, computer simulation,
and scientists huddled over shards
of disturbingly marked bone.

But the artist who trickles colored sand
on this wooden floor today dwells clearly
in a peaceful universe, his hand guided by
impulse that resembles the kindness of animals
who raise their heads and tilt their ears
into the wind countless times a day,
then go back to grazing. The perfect
circles and lines, then the shadings
that spill from his hand, seem to carve
his painting deep into the floor. "We only think
we know where we've been," he says quietly,
spilling us into his version of time. A flick of his wrist,
the arc of his arm, and all the murky weather
we may have brought here disappears into dunes
of color. Borders made flush. Lines deliberate
and fine as laser cuts. "There are maps to the past
that have never been read," he says, cupping
cool green sand in his palm as though he had just
drawn it from a well after days of walking.

I look at the small bowls of rose, aqua, gold,
flame, delphinium blue, and have to turn away—
how many eons in the history of this dun-colored earth

did it take to leave such a palette? His painting
thrives now, tiered walls and hills, elk and ibis,
cured hides, bright yarns, and milled wheat
shimmering in its borders. "We only think we know
what we leave for others to find," he says,
sweeping the finished piece into a heap of sand
that suddenly is dun-colored again
and vibrates like a struck gong.

Contract

Sometimes we
put aside the big questions
if we can have a few hours in thinned air
full of snow's breathing,
full of trees breathing beneath
snow, the weight of winter
so entrenched we can
feel the whole earth
stilled. And the mountain
seems to accept what we've
slashed into it, chain saws
whining through summer air
so in winter we can claim a freedom
our bodies were not designed for.
We racket down its sides,
our inefficient uprightness
carried back up on cables drilled
into rock. Beneath the fiberglass
and metals, the custom-fitted plastics,
the graphics and pomp we clamp
to our fragile feet, the mountain
keeps a poise that resists
without rejecting us.

But if we're willing to receive it
softly, through the fragile essence
of our feet, and open ourselves
to its dips and gullies, its glades,
its silence—if we are willing to absorb
the force of a solitude
that makes us disappear, the mountain
opens in us a third eye to find
the places that will let us fly
safely and land without breaking
our new contract with gravity—
we, whose young remain helpless

longer than young ermine or deer—
we whom gravity weights and slows
even in our prime—small wonder
we're not extinct. The mountain,
though it remembers, allows us
to be gods for a time without doing harm.

Among the Mysteries

At one end of the sky, the comet
last seen by pharaohs
noses into view like an animal
so steeped, so safe
in its wildness it can only
be friendly
or at least impartial,
laying its tail across our hemisphere's
troubled horizons

while opposite, the entire
moon is swallowed by
shadow, mud-and-water earth
sliding like a wing across
her flank—tonight
she must feel a chill of swamp
and forest, must feel
rank sea breath as a disturbance
of dust—tonight she is smudged
and accompanied

and I, threading myself
through binoculars, grow
weightless, strung between
headlong comet and Leda moon.
The fire I've built in this
dented trash-can lid
and Petunia, who has emerged
from the tall grass to press, purring
and mammalian against my knee,

are fixed points in the hurtling
night, earth and moon
pulling six billion horoscopes into new
alignments, the wake
of their entanglement, a great

wheel turning in every house of
work, love, money, health

while the comet, whose tidings
will soon veer from
the world's eye for another
four thousand years, draws
a larger axis: who, on this acre
someday no longer desert,
will be its next witness?

Tonight I am message
and impulse, groundless
yet moist in the eye. I am
catch in the throat. I am cat
meshing again with
night grasses
and fire eating itself
to the ground, as the moon
shrugs our shadow from
her flank, edgy and
new-minted—insistent, as she
resumes her shape, that nothing
has changed.

Equatorial

You were going to ask: and where
are the lilacs? but what about
the empty water bottles,
the sweaty pesos you blindly
handed over for the journey
and the suitcases left behind on the pier?
What about the avocado sprinkled
with lime so strong it cures raw fish
in minutes, and the grainy local cheese
you were offered after the boat
was pulled ashore? You lean
against a palm that needs 140 inches of rain a year
while heavy-billed birds with glints of
yellow in their wings
shatter the sky, their voices
crow-raucous and combative. Bougainvilleas
cascade from high trees—
a come-hither color, a throaty pink
that looks injected—and even the rocks sprout
leaves on top of moss on top of leaves—what good
would lilacs do you here? They remain, like
your flashlight and underwear, on the mainland
of the past—four decades behind you, to be exact,
beside the house where you grew up—do they
still scent the Midwestern June nights
with a promise of muted light, the almost-silence
of chiffon? Once, on a visit, you
sought a pale glimpse of purple,
the thought of which provoked
an ambush of longing in your throat,
but a new house had been built
where the wild garden used to be—
an eight-foot cedar fence imprisoned you
for good from anyone, past or present,
who might have time to sip iced tea
on the back porch, note that fleeting,

crushable scent, and think about the future
you never imagined as this headlong rush
through seasons and time zones,
this play of bounty minus most of
what you thought was yours
to take with you.

And My Life Wandered On

The rock I bumped over while learning
to drive remains lodged in the sandy road to the landing.
Every time, I glimpse someone I was.

Now a strong wind has found
its way into these woods, where it
rarely goes, riled by carbons

from other latitudes—whitecaps
trouble our summer bay, and old cleats
on the wooden dock one by one let go of the boats.

The long life slouches in the doorway I've become
and asks if I've ever stepped into a new landscape
without dragging along the one I live in. . . .

Maybe once. In Bolivia. On a plain
tucked high in the Andes, sky and land
a seamless sheet of grey, the air

thrilling in its scarcity, peasants
wandering among their cows and digging at roots
in a fretful, indecisive sleet—

because the sky was so much itself, a vast equilibrium
near the equator that lowered its one long season
like a dome over the ruins, the huts, the generations

of cooking fires sending their smoke into air that withheld
nearly everything. For a few moments
I was a seed, a mistake, perhaps

a shrug or a shift of wind
and the place of my birth a pinprick,
an ace drawn from the pack and laid facedown.

Mind Returns to Find Itself Absent

I looked into the room that no longer
looked at me. In one of the many lives
I hadn't lived, city lights blurred the stars

but not the buildings, their clean lines, their roots invisible.

Now my windows let go of the room's colors—
I mean really let them *go*

as though they were sugar dissolving into the night—
spines of books, lamplight, kilim blues and maroons—
a history that happened to be mine

without retaining a single significant image

as though I had already given them away,
the spaces carved by their absence
waiting, impartial, for the next stranger,

the memory of another life—
a house by the sea, its single porch light

drawing small fish momentarily to the surface
or tall grasses in a field, grasses
taller than a person, blowing

in the dark—I've never seen them
but I know how they sound.

III

Mind Trades Shadows with the Clouds

A neighbor's horses have been
moved to the field outside my study—
seven chestnuts, their shades of brown
blending, parting, forming new
densities of brown. They drift
across their acre like a slow-moving front.

At times I've had the unfamiliar
sense my life has walls I can
run my hands along in the dark,
a dwelling I seem to have to myself
at last, its astonishing silence,
my quarrels with former selves
having faded to an occasional
skirmish. I assume nothing.

Even through closed eyes I can see
the land filling with shadows,
and endlessly above it, light
older than anyone can imagine collides
without dissolving against
whatever appears in its path.
Some change is gathering beyond
where I can see, its shadow growing long,
unrecognizable, before a lowering sun.

To the human eye, the drifting horses
have nothing to do with the freewheeling
light. But if their legs allowed them
to lower themselves and doze
too long, whole worlds
would tip to destruction—the veins
and gut with their intricate barters
of gasses and proteins, the alto pipes

through which oxygen rearranges itself
into carbons, the tireless furnace of the heart.
Their brown backs soak up the November sun
which calms them—they have hardly moved
for the last hour, though if spooked they would
explode into their long history of flight.

Patient

My neighbor's brother, rail thin
and quiet, drives an hour from town
to walk into the desert with Kiki,
the ancient sheltie, whose slight body
grows weightless as she begins
to trot, easing the age from her legs.
What will sand yield today? Something
like tides keeps turning buried things to the sun.
Devil's claw. Vertebra from calf or coyote.
Yucca pod of seeds about to race away.

The sand has blown into swells, ripples,
stilled waves over layers of rock.
I imagine Joe disturbs nothing; I'm the one
who runs a hand along them in my mind.
Spent bullet casings. Broken glass, all edge
and glare, like my brain feels when locked
onto a slot machine in the casino of itself.

He lives near the airport, where parking lots
and four-lanes and dealerships devour
whole city blocks, their flags
garish over the din of polished cars.
He drifts past my window, the silence
washing over him like surf,
his soul expanding in his narrow chest
and going a little ahead of him—a prow,
a beacon—with the brown-and-white dog
who doesn't know she's old. Today, although
the waves receded lifetimes ago, the sand offers
an entire clam, petrified, big enough to
fill the palm with the warmed stone of itself.

At the End of Daylight Savings

sunlight glares off the road like trumpet sound.
Birds still thicken the air with messages
at dawn, a telegraphy that fills the morning

too full for one pair of ears—
one might as well listen with the whole body.
And then take that listening

to the base of the mountain whose creases
are dusted with snow already sure
of its place before the months lengthen

and darken, each crystal soon to be fed by
clouds and swells of wind that will drive it
into deeper configurations.

Then the mountain will glow faintly
even at night—especially at night—sculpture,
apparition, an *is-ness* hovering beyond each

dormant bush and distracted eye. Even now,
even those who have never been on speaking terms
with God have no choice but to open

to something that sears and consoles
beneath jackets newly unpacked for the season: how clouds
and their leavings change the light on the mountain

but not the shape of its silence.

Hole in the Mind Filling with the Present

Light and wind—warm
in some seasons, in others
cut with indifferent
crystal—the child you were
came often to sit among leaf
rustlings and dappled sun,

the hole in her mind,
like the minds of everyone,
a necessary blindness

that began to close imperceptibly
at first, the seasons
turning, four tableaux
of grey, green, blue, or golden
light, a continuous wheel.

Over the years you took out
whatever was in your pockets and
set it down. The stories in which you
had to be the hero. The risks
you had longed for.

Now time has slowed
again, as it did
when you had a mother
and a father, tall, one on each side,

even as it brings a rushing sound.
Pine needles falling
and tree limbs broken among

the trees. Your body, now
clothed thinly
in skin, filling with
holes—only something

porous like this can feel
what has always been wind.

A Visible Life

The mind is a small city
whose street signs show me

what I already know. Cafés, theaters,
the little shop for incense—they offer

useful pleasures. Between late snows
that cover Kachina Peak, the new season

takes its time; the sun lights vertical acres
of crystal while new green presses

out of beaten bark. In that high country
anyone's heart can fly. But something remains

beyond me, and the tired grass I land upon
doesn't bring me closer—this winter grass

that is unconcerned about what will be
left of it after the thaw.

Mind Out of Season

A certain absence that is not-mind
sits quietly. Gathering around itself, as it
often does, waves of patience
that weave into a kind of trance.
Something not-effort.
Something that precedes words
and outlasts them. Receptive, unhurried, it rocks
in November sun, grateful for the thin
gold broth. Grateful for the hours
that remain. Turning cheek and brow
to the light even as earth itself
turns away. It gives little thought
to its recalcitrant limbs, the onslaught of effort
when it rises at last to go in. Pomegranates
plucked weeks ago and halved on a plate
offer seeds that ripen still, ambrosial,
beneath the damaged leather of their skin. Mind
perches at the table's other side, edgy,
driven in by weather. Pansies thrive in a bowl
before the largest window while light weakens outside—
all winter the thin light and snow, and that improbable
purple. Deep. Midnight. Befriending.

The Seasons Only Borrow Us

Here is the moon, its silver hum
filling the valley. Here are the wings
of the hummingbird joined in their velocity
at first light, cloud of wing
suspended beside the column
of ruby water. Here are the beaten
boards of the deck finally emerging
from old snow, and the sun
sharpening itself on the cold
stone of the ridge—

all day, it scoops more snow
from Kachina Peak to reveal
grey rock and the few
stunted leaves that can breathe
in thin air. No one
walks those tightrope
heights after the last skier
has relinquished whatever bravado
moved him to leave his
lit rooms at dawn and spend
all day in wind dark with ice.

Here is the apple tree—
its snow of new blossoms—
and old snow shrinking from the ridge
where I, too, climbed with
skis on my back and water barely
unfrozen enough to drink.
Already I'm up there again, this time
with compass and binoculars, seeking
a familiar house and vanished deck,
tree emptied of fruit,
glass column emptied of rubies.

Progress on the Subject of Immensity

Light is laying waste the heavens . . .
but how does one lay waste to
absence? *The heavens.* Euphemism

for container that is no container
at all. Antithesis of *place.*
My thoughts disappear into
a blue that makes

this sand, this late-summer
grass, the neighbors' white barn
and red horse trailer unmistakably

part of the earth's curve—
earth, a pebble. And I am
perched upon it, glad
that what's before me is not concrete

or cinder block or steel, but the tans and
greens one would see from outer space.
Petunia notes none of this,

arranging herself like an ornament
on the desk before me—she, too,
is *the heavens* in her unique
black-and-whiteness—just what loops

and detours of ancestry produced
those asymmetrical black
smudges on her chin and left paw?

Perhaps light lays
some kind of waste if
nightfall contains us within a boundary
we might touch if we had to

but if I sent myself into that dark
as I do into this blue, I might
discover I had no body

at all, and the stars no longer
where their light tells us they are.
Like this brown and green late-
summer desert, the barn and trailer,

the birds pecking my pomegranates
to shreds, and me and Petunia
here in the house. Today, there isn't

a single cloud or contrail or whisper
of haze. It's impossible
not to consider that blue, that
clearly infinite but decisive blue

as *presence*. Something planned.

Mind Gives Up an Attempt to Describe the Scent of New Paper

In the prolonged swathe of color
that deepens after summer, like a long
exhalation saved for the shortened
days, a honeyed yellow travels
toward the tips of leaves—this
is how heavy summer lifts yet again
from the mind that is quickened
as though starting school
with a clean tablet whose smell
everyone can remember.

I used to dream of living here. Now I do
but it's hard not to slip from a place one loves
when one's still in it. Today the whole
canyon is aflame with the scent
of leaves that aren't so much dead
as crisp, blowing gold over dark asphalt.
Again I taste the longing that set
its sights on these mountains,
this light and omnivorous sky,
the wild weather that is drawn here.

I used to dream of being
engulfed in fame. What on earth
did I mean? Here. Instead. Something
that holds light long after the light is gone.

Nova That Suddenly

blooms through binoculars
may be taking in our smallest
comings and goings, now that earth
is its closest neighbor in the frozen sky—
iced, magnified, nimbus of long-spent light,
it delivers a birth across a million
light-years to confound the present eye

and a possible new link between man
and ape has just been lifted from
its sheath of earth—a pelvis
too narrow to pass a head encasing
the circuitry of human thought
and a set of shapely finger bones,
opposable thumbs, prediction of a hand
that will lift tools, throw spears, wear rings—
this, too, has taken a million years to emerge from
a universe locked away beneath our feet—

so two more secrets penetrate our slender strip
of light and breathable air, stopping us cold
in the midst of negotiations with calendar
and clock, the white noise of longing
and a shape-shifting creator who
may dwell deep inside us,
may dwell deep beyond our line of sight.

Without Steel or Fire

Ever since school and even before
I have run my fingers along
the borders on maps. *To look at a river*
made of time and water is to see
the first cracks in the jigsaw
earth has become. Now inked lines
unfurl beneath my thumb, each boundary
an opportunity to straddle two countries at once,
to ride the vowels of two dialects.
I dream myself, beyond the stamps
on my passport, a citizen of the world,
as though I were river carving its way
by persuasion alone through rock.
I dream myself silt stirred up and rootless,
knowing the taste of each nation
through the root vegetables it yields.
Once Africa nestled right into
South America. Yam against yucca.
Now the river between them
is a sea that spans four time zones,
its tireless fingers against the muscled earth
still working at the knots. I dream myself
harmless as the crane or butterfly
that travels thousands of miles to follow
the changing position of the sun,
irrefutable as the salmon that swim
upriver to spawn and die, their journeys
blurring even the fortified borders.

Mudra

How was I like the pinecone
that outlived me?
Shingled, yes, with
aspects of a singular life—
certain wounds and the impulse
to cover them, a preference
for winter, an attraction to
altitude and stone. . . .

We were nourished in part by sun
and melted snow
and probably left a trace of
pitch now and then
on someone else's skin.

Prickly? I tried to
hide it, to be milkweed
or dandelion fluff, and
often willed myself
to disappear on the wind.

But it's the shape of the hand
curved from thumb to middle
finger as it holds the pinecone
end to end—

or rather, the shape of air
the thumb and finger make
alongside, the pleasing sensation
of that shaping, and then

the awareness of one's own hand as it
shapes the air alongside—
that I entered the world hoping
others might feel: the shape
of themselves when they
found themselves alongside me.

Two

The taste of October on your shoulders
distracts me from your reasonable gestures
of seduction. *I have in my throat one*
word, but I don't know the sound of it,
only that it feels like breath along
my cheek. Or a hand over mine.
You might think your kiss and a few
endearments have softened me;
it's the word I don't know
to which I seem to surrender.
I find myself on a strange
path that involves my hands
and, yes, your skin, which becomes
landscape for the search. A word
surrounded by phantom sound. Dunes
beneath my palms. A string of syllables
with no beginning. Something large in the chest,
wings in the solar plexus, goose bumps
riding the arms. A warmth like bronze
and then a hint of burning leaves—
smoke—something out there
wants to be near the soul that is mine
and it has a name. I have never
thought of God with any sense
of harbor. Maybe you haven't either.
Now I seem to have woven us into this dance
between frost and fire. Maybe the silence
that holds me at bay from
what I've been told is the Divine
is the silence that fills my word.

Still, Small

Silence. An almost-
voice that needs no name,
asks nothing. Fanned in solitude
during long seasons when the known self
retreats to a chilled sleep.

It lives on air but adores the elements—
earth, fossil, water, crystal, every
spectrum color, shell, stone,
and memory.

It's been known to pry open
the future's empty rooms and put pieces
of world back in—blue of iris, bite of espresso,
early sun, a single feather floating down—until word
greets body, bypassing every edifice
God is said to dwell in.

Against grief
it erects a tent in the rain
of knives. Or can break the stone
of no-feeling with a current that reaches
through cracks and flows toward the open,
the felt landscape of fresh, unbidden thought.

Consider Desire

When we pause at the near edge
of memory or invention and elect
not to venture further, we don't
consider that invisible journeys, too,
leave dried mud and grass on our shoes;
that one can dream of waltzing with
a stranger, following every
subtle lead, and wake up happy

or be consoled by a fragrant loaf
mentioned briefly in a poem;
that the bowl of desert once held
an ocean we can borrow any time
we cup our minds around it, like hands
around spinning clay. Once I halted
on a winter street, noticing the turquoise

stone had slipped from the center of my ring.
I reversed my steps and searched for hours,
peering downward for a bit of sky,
seeing every crevice in the dark
pavement, every sodden leaf and twig.
I fingered the empty bezel, sky
filling my mind. Luminous. Parachute of blue.

Notes

"Equinox": The italicized language is borrowed from the first two lines of "Who Will Buy Me an Orange?" by José Garostiza, trans. Rachel Benson, in Stephen Tapscott, ed., *Twentieth-Century Latin American Poetry: A Bilingual Anthology*, Texas Pan American Series (Austin: University of Texas Press, 1996).

"The Guises of the Mind": This poem is modeled after Jane Hirshfield's poem, "The Lives of the Heart," which appears in her volume, *The Lives of the Heart* (New York: Harper Perennial, 1997).

"Don't Sleep Yet": The title of this poem is a phrase borrowed from the first line of "Rainy Night" by Juana de Ibarbourou, trans. Sophie Cabot Black and Maria Negroni, in Stephen Tapscott, ed., *Twentieth-Century Latin American Poetry: A Bilingual Anthology*, Texas Pan American Series (Austin: University of Texas Press, 1996).

"The Story I Need": The italicized language is borrowed from the first line of "Poem of the Girl from Velázquez" by Ricardo Molinari, trans. Inés Probert, in Stephen Tapscott, ed., *Twentieth-Century Latin American Poetry: A Bilingual Anthology*, Texas Pan American Series (Austin: University of Texas Press, 1996).

"Beautiful / This Morning, No Myth Felt Lacking": The title of this poem is borrowed from the first two lines of "Diminutive" by Carlos Drummond de Andrade, trans. Virginia de Araújo, in Stephen Tapscott, ed., *Twentieth-Century Latin American Poetry: A Bilingual Anthology*, Texas Pan American Series (Austin: University of Texas Press, 1996).

"Amnesia": The epigraph is from "Lamento" by Tomas Tranströmer, in *Friends, You Drank Some Darkness: Three Swedish Poets, Harry Martinson, Gunnar Ekelöf, and Tomas Tranströmer*, trans. Robert Bly (Boston: Beacon Press, 1975).

"Equatorial": The italicized language is borrowed from the first line of "I'm Explaining a Few Things" by Pablo Neruda, trans. Nathaniel Tarn, in Stephen Tapscott, ed., *Twentieth-Century Latin American Poetry: A Bilingual Anthology*, Texas Pan American Series (Austin: University of Texas Press, 1996).

"Progress on the Subject of Immensity": The italicized language is borrowed from the first line of "Native Stone" by Octavio Paz, trans. Muriel Rukeyser, in Stephen Tapscott, ed., *Twentieth-Century Latin American Poetry: A Bilingual Anthology*, Texas Pan American Series (Austin: University of Texas Press, 1996).

"Without Steel or Fire": The first italicized passage is borrowed from the first line of "Ars Poetica" by Jorge Luis Borges, trans. W. S. Merwin. The second is borrowed from the first line of "My Last Name" by Nicolás Guillén, trans. Robert Márquez and David Arthur McMurray. Both poems are in Stephen Tapscott, ed., *Twentieth-Century Latin American Poetry: A Bilingual Anthology*, Texas Pan American Series (Austin: University of Texas Press, 1996).

"Two": The first italicized passage is borrowed from the first line of "To Poetry" by Carlos Pellicer, trans. Alexandra Migoya. The second is borrowed from the first line of "One Word" by Gabriela Mistral, trans. Doris Dana. Both poems are in Stephen Tapscott, ed., *Twentieth-Century Latin American Poetry: A Bilingual Anthology*, Texas Pan American Series (Austin: University of Texas Press, 1996).